Project Influence and Leadership

Building Rapport in Teams

Project Influence and Leadership

Leadership

Building Rapport in Teams

Michael Nir

Sapir Publishing, Boston, MA

Fourth Edition © 2017 by Michael Nir

ATTENTION CORPORATIONS, UNIVERSITIES, COLLEGES AND PROFFESIONAL ORGANIZATIONS!

Quantity discounts are available on bulk purchases of this book and the book can be completely customized for your organization to fit specific needs.

Contact us at **sapir@sapir-cs.com**

i

Accolades

*"There is no doubt that the knowledge that is communicated in Nir's work can **radically change the trajectory of careers and businesses**. That much can be understood from trawling though business literature or through reading this **excellent** digest that is brought into the real world with an **expert's insight**.*
***Thanks for sharing** your personal experience with us Michael."* ...

*"Thanks writer for this **amazing book**. This little hand book gave me insights I now use every day with my clients. **So useful, thank you!**"* ...

*"anyone involved in business as it teaches you how **to identify personalities and how to influence** them to get the job done without making them feel manipulated or overrun"*...

*"I like it and **recommend** it to others who are working in a matrix environments and who wish to **motivate, communicate and influence**"* ...

*"Specifically the model at the end of the book is **enlightening and helpful** - addressing various stakeholders' personalities. **It influenced me** and I hope I can influence others.... :)."* ...

*"A well rounded, clear, logically structured, bottoms-up, **succinct and entertaining** guide to every-day organizational leadership and communication issues. While each chapter can be expanded into a book in itself, the **beauty of this book is in its effective breakdown** of complicated issues into simple and executable strategies and tactics. A must read for any mid-level manager (and above)"...*

*"I found that I could relate to the first chapters a little too well - not just in learning new **influencing** tips for myself, but also in understanding **how others have manipulated**, er... **influenced**, me in the past"* ...

Preface

Imagine that you master the magic of influence and get people to do what you want? Imagine that you have a clear path of how to accomplish it. You have made the right decision, once you have read me you will not believe that you ever managed without the concepts within! With the knowledge in this book at your disposal, you will possess the secret magical formula that eludes so many others – the recipe to unveiling the magic of Leadership and INFLUENCE WITHOUT AUTHORITY.

Distilled and tested by the author in this succinct guide and unearthed on its pages are the proven steps for your success.

Michael

Boston, 2017

Reader Tools

For your enhanced reader experience I use the following interactive tools in the book:

Remember scrolls: summarize concepts discussed to assist information retention

Thinking alerts: are highlighted regions in the text that emphasize important take-aways to use in the 'real' world. I recommend reading these twice and taking notes for future reference

Case Study paragraphs: *Signify stories that bring to life the issues discussed in the book.*

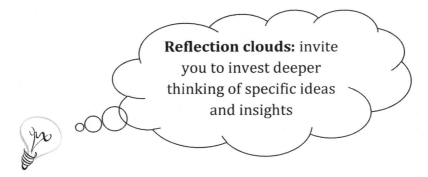

Reflection clouds: invite you to invest deeper thinking of specific ideas and insights

"Sometimes you eat the bear,
..and sometimes the bear eats you"
(Ethan and Joel Coen)

"Sometimes you eat the bear,

..and sometimes the bear eats you"

(Ethan and Joel Coen)

Contents

CHAPTER

ONE

Introduction

Introduction

Hiking with two friends toward a glacier in the Alaskan range in Denali National Park, we were camping on a small gravel shore line near a lake . I was in my tent, exchanging my wet clothes for more wet clothes, because in Alaska you're always wet; As I was taking off my pants, I heard Barack, who at the time was standing near the tents enjoying the afternoon drizzle, saying, "Guys, there's a bear here."

Barack was somewhat of a clown and not someone to be taken seriously. This time, however, the tone of his voice was different. The third time he repeated his warning, I started believing that maybe there was a bear out there. So I replied, "Yes, of course, ... you mean that there is a bear across the lake, on the hill far away..." His answer was quick and unequivocal. "No! the bear is on this side of the lake." The trouble with 'this side of the lake' was,.. that it was only 12 feet away from my tent.

Just to be certain, I asked Barack, "What do you mean this side of the lake? There are only 12 feet separating us and the lake." Barack didn't reply;

instead, he started following the procedure for close bear encounters.

As implied from the traveler's guide to the Alaskan outback, the procedure for close bear encounters is somewhat confusing. The approach for handling a black bear encounter is different, and to an extent opposite, from the approach for a grizzly bear encounter. Black bears can be frightened by aggressive behavior and will pursue you if you're running away. The directive is to stand your ground and put on your most fearsome face. Grizzlies, on the other hand, are not easily intimidated; however, they're not very good climbers. When facing a grizzly, it is better to climb a tree or stand your ground with a not-so-aggressive face.

If the grizzly decides to charge, it is recommended to stand your ground, but most likely, it is better to play dead. Playing dead means lying on your stomach with your hands on your neck and your head hidden beneath your hands. Your hope is that, at most, the grizzly will chew on your leg because bears do not eat dead meat.

The challenge with the guidelines is that an adolescent grizzly might look blackish, and a mature female grizzly bear may sometimes appear a bit blonde similar to a black bear. The obvious way to verify the gender is usually not applicable while the bear is awake and not advisable when the bear is asleep.

Barack—making a swift decision on the gender and type of the bear —decided this was an adolescent grizzly and started saying in a commanding voice, "Go away bear!" This command, or wish, was accompanied by a slow waving of the hands above the head. I will add that Barack was speaking Hebrew, and we were all very hopeful that this specific grizzly was multilingual.

Erez, that was also busy in his tent, and I, joined Barak on the shoreline to show camaraderie. So, there we were: three wet, miserable, and scared-to-death hikers looking at a full-size grizzly not 12 feet away. Two of us in our underwear and one of us was aiming a small canister of pepper spray toward the bear. The bear was judging the situation with what appeared to be an amused bearish glance; it seemed that he was educated in Semitic languages since he continued treading on.

He was probably convinced that either we were not edible, were not kosher, or that three grown men, two of whom were wearing underwear looking at him and speaking in a strange language, were probably carrying some contagious disease and it was better for him to leave them be.

Good thing we were not forced to use the pepper spray because Erez, in the heat of the skirmish, forgot to remove the safety latch.

The vividness of this face-to-face bear encounter is still as powerful for me today as it was when it happened over 20 years ago.

A few years back, I was preparing a keynote about how to communicate, convince, and influence stakeholders. In modern business, and specifically in the global environment, hierarchies are blurred, the lines of command are unclear, and the method by which to motivate and influence stakeholders is to an extent based on persuasion and the ability to impact without any specific power of retribution or reward.

In this sense, I find a genuine resemblance between the business scenario and my personal bear encounter.

I utilize, therefore, the example of the bear encounter in the context of convincing stakeholders in an organization. In the same way that in the great Alaskan outdoors, without a rifle, one must persuade and coax a bear not to attack, in the modern global organization, one must use methods for influencing, convincing, and other non-confrontational techniques to achieve one's goals.

This book presents a synthesis of the various concepts of convincing, leadership, and influence. They are depicted through three fundamentals:

1. stakeholder management;
2. leadership style; and
3. communication and influence style.

These three fundamentals can also be seen in the context of moving from outside inward. We start by analyzing the stakeholder community, by and large, discussing methods to manage stakeholders and influence them. We then move to specific leadership techniques that are useful when leading our teams;

these are explained with the practice of situational leadership. We conclude with presenting communication strategies to increase our influence on individuals. All the techniques presented **must be accompanied by a mindset change**; it takes more than merely implementing knowledgeable techniques to increase ones influence and leadership aptitude.

I wish you success in increasing your influence without authority skills.

Reflect who are your 'organizational bears', what are you doing to lead and influence them?

CHAPTER TWO

It's Destiny -
We Are All Bears in the Matrix

It's Destiny -
We Are All Bears in the Matrix

The modern business, big and small, is typically organized in a matrix structure. The matrix organizational structure became popular in the 1980s; it then receded in popularity in the 1990s and regained widespread acceptance in the 2000s. At present, the matrix organization is ubiquitous. Most global consulting firms, when asked to reorganize businesses, select the matrix organization as their preferred structure.

The reasons are obvious. In a global, complex, multinational organization, the matrix makes sense. Moreover, the matrix organization is considered cheaper in terms of resource utilization, and it provides a robust network for information-sharing.

Project managers might argue that the savings brought about by moving the organization to a matrix structure are never actualized. Indeed, from the project and product perspective, the matrix organization introduces considerable complexity.

Confusion and conflict are inherent in the matrix structure because department lines are blurred, hierarchies are often unclear, and business objectives are achieved through hard-to-accomplish cooperation and collaboration.

According to the Project Management Body of Knowledge (PMBOK®), by the Project Management Institute (PMI®), the matrix is an organizational structure in which the project manager shares responsibility with the functional managers for assigning priorities and for directing the work of persons assigned to the project.

In the complex matrix structure, it is possible to find a project manager from procurement, leading an initiative together with representatives from IT, human resources, logistics, operations, and manufacturing departments. Similarly, a project manager from product development, at some point, will have team members from operations, quality, engineering, research and development, and sales and marketing departments. These are just two of the many possibilities of integration and collaboration in the matrix environment.

Along with the sought after flexibility and adaptability of the matrix organization, some challenges are present. Because employees have various tasks that are part of their designated roles and responsibilities, they will not necessarily support and assist others. Very similar to the bears in the Alaskan outback, **the employees in the matrix organization have to be coaxed, influenced, and persuaded to support a project initiative**.

Common complaints often heard from individuals in the matrix organization can include to:

1. How can I possibly promote my activities when the entire team does not report to me?

2. I am the leader of quality in this activity, but I cannot influence my colleagues to accept my professional opinion.

3. I have no resources, but I have a lot of activities requiring resources.

4. I am responsible for integrating the product, but the software developers are not helping with fixing the bugs.

5. I am managing a change project initiated by human resources and my contact in IT has no time to help me with the reporting structure update.

These complaints illustrate the key obstacles of promoting initiatives in the matrix organization: Support can't be taken for granted.

Not only junior employees face with these complexities, but high-level executives also find it difficult to promote initiatives in the global matrix organization. At times it seems that the work to be completed is lost within the matrix. When executives use their legitimate organizational power, they discover that it is complicated to enforce orders in the ever-changing flexible matrix.

As mentioned, rather than command and control management, the **matrix organization structure requires leadership and influence**. It is no wonder that in the last decade, training for communication soft skills has rocketed in popularity. As a matter of fact, influence without authority as a soft skills aptitude is a prerequisite to achieving results in the matrix structure. As a result, leadership and influence without authority have become a major driver for organizational excellence in the last 10 or 15 years.

A few years ago, I participated in a company-wide presentation delivered by the president and CEO of a global organization with over 110,000 employees. He was visiting a small manufacturing and production site for hi-tech medical equipment. The entire organization required restructuring and the CEO was on a tour presenting his vision. At one point in his presentation, he took a personal tone and in a genuine plea to the participants said, "I can't do the change alone. I need your help."

This candid message is a great example of how the old days of command and control mechanisms are gone. They are no longer acceptable in the global corporation. This example shows that even the CEO of a highly reputable organization could appeal to the employees of a small and remote plant for their support in leading the change. For me, this typifies the shift of power we are experiencing over the last years. It is no longer acceptable behavior to employ positional power to secure results; furthermore, people who have and use positional power aren't viewed positively.

I have used influence and leadership interchangeably, and there is a difference between them. What is influence and how does it differ from leadership?

➢ *Influence is the process of using power to get someone to do something.*

➢ *Leadership is the capacity to enlist the aid and support of others in the accomplishment of a common task.*

Considering these definitions, it is clear that each leadership effort is also an influence effort; however not each influence attempt is also a leadership effort.

While influence and leadership are processes, power is the resource we use in order to carry them out.

Further explaining the process of power, we can identify several types of power within an organization: position power, coercive power, resource power, information power, association power, expert power, and personal power.

- **Position power** can also be described as formal or legitimate power. However formal, legitimate organization power is in most cases based on some degree of coercion or, in other words, there is always the possibility of using force to encourage behavior. Position power can include any combination of the following types of power: coercive, resource, information, and association.

- **Coercive power** is fear-based. This is the power of superior force, and it is the power of a manager to punish. As mentioned above, with the advent of the 21st century enlightened management theories of empowerment and self-management, coercive power has lost its legitimacy. In most cases and in many organizations, it is not considered best-practice to utilize coercive power; rather people need to be bought-in, influenced, and convinced.

- **Resource power** is based on control over resources, both people and material. Resource power is evident in matrix organizations where functional managers who control resources are able to decide which of them will be appointed to which activities and projects. In one of the hi-tech organizations for which I consult, the line managers, who are also the technical leaders, use their power over department resources to make sure that the projects are following their priorities. The project organization suffers and the project managers are struggling to complete projects based on the plans they have developed.

- **Information power** is based on control and access to information. For example:

  o Consider the case of the engineering department not sharing know-how on some process with manufacturing to keep controlling a certain domain.

  o The IT department controlling spreadsheet automation applications to deride a rollout of a global resource planning tool.

  o The finance department maintaining invoice information in manual hard copy folders that prevent online access.

In all these examples the control over access to the information provides the owner information with power.

- **Association power**, also known as referral power, is the power of having access or a perceived relationship to someone who has power. This can also be described as "name dropping," which carries a negative connotation. By explicitly or implicitly creating a link to someone who has power, one builds power through association. Association power is usually less tangible than other types of power but is no less potent. The VP of supply chain might be hesitant to command the compliance of one of his subordinates if he believes that this subordinate is good friends with the CEO. Association power can also be considered a personal type of power.

- **Expert power** is the power of having specific expertise, know-how, or competency. This is the power of being the only one who can fix a critical machine in the production line or who knows how to sell to a specific client or knows certain functionalities and operations of the product or who knows how to support the application during on-site visits, and so on. Expert power differs from information power because information power originates from outside the individual and the power arises from being able to protect access to the information. On the other hand, expert power resides within the person who has the expertise.

- **Personal power** is the ability to gain power through charisma, persuasion, and convincing. Influence without authority is based on personal informal power. Leadership, according to the definition above, can be based on a mix of personal power with other types of power. Sometimes leadership is more about personal informal power and sometimes it is not. Expert power is a type of personal power.

Dimensions of personal power: Personal power consists of individual personality proficiencies. The capacity to learn and develop dimensions in creating personal power is often the center of debate. Some claim that these abilities are inborn and impossible to develop; others assert that coaching and mentoring can create great change in individuals. The truth is **somewhere in between**. To an extent, a few elements of **informal power are indeed inborn**; **however, other elements can be developed and honed**. Notwithstanding, if we did believe the assertion made by the first group, then mentors, coaches, and entire human resource departments would become superfluous.

Accepting that in the modern organization results are based more on personal power than on position power is actually admitting that, to a degree, we are all bears in a matrix organization in the sense that sometimes we are influencing others and sometimes we are being influenced by others. Similar to bears, we can decide who to support in which activities the same way others decide whether to assist us wholeheartedly in our projects and tasks. Analogously, in order to influence the stakeholders, we sometimes have to talk slowly and wave our hands over our shoulders to get attention and support.

> **Thinking alert:**
> Since we rarely can obtain the necessary positional power over all the resources who contribute to our efforts, it is crucial to develop influence that is based on personal

The remainder of this book will present a **framework for acquiring personal informal power in order to influence and lead within the matrix**

global organization. Chapter 2 offers a discussion about stakeholder management, the notion that stakeholders differ in their perceptions, and some **strategies for influencing**. Chapter 3 introduces the concept of **situational leadership within the framework of active listening and empathy** as a method to acquire informal power. Chapter 4 focuses on **alignment with target audience and analysis of communication style preferences** in order to achieve maximum impact when communicating, thus increasing informal power.

CHAPTER

THREE

Loving the Champion Bear

Loving the Champion Bear

In her children's book *Bear Feels Sick*, Karma Wilson describes how the hero bear is sick and playing on his friends to cater to his needs. His lovable smallish friends help out and perform many chores, including cooking, preparing tea, and keeping the sick bear company. The bear remains ill throughout the book until, suddenly, he is miraculously cured.

Most of the book describes how his charade convinces even the otherwise envious raven, the badgering badger, and the ever-so-efficient mole to continuously and wholeheartedly tend to his needs. While I don't know if Wilson considered her book an analogy to influencing stakeholders in the matrix organization, this book teaches us an important lesson: the significance of stakeholder leadership. The shrewd bear skillfully identifies the stakeholders, analyzes their attitudes, and convinces them in a passive-aggressive way to help while he is relaxing in his sick bed.

Much can be learned from this story, and this chapter presents a discussion about stakeholder leadership. It investigates the concept that stakeholders differ in their perceptions, and it introduces a strategy for influence.

> ➤ *Stakeholders are persons or organizations (e.g., customers, sponsors, performing organizations, or the public) actively involved in a project or whose interests might be affected positively or negatively by the execution or completion of a project. A stakeholder might also exert influence over the project and its deliverables (PMBOK®).*

In this book, I will be using the term "stakeholder" in a broader sense, i.e., any individual who can affect your work and activities, which can be non-project related.

Keeping the Nice Bears Close to You

The first step in building support among the greater stakeholder community is identifying the various stakeholder groups and individuals affecting the project/activities and analyzing their attitudes. Identifying stakeholders can be completed alone or with a small team. Because analyzing stakeholders is a sensitive undertaking, it makes sense to perform the activity with the kernel project team, ensuring that the output of the analysis remains within the team.

The objective of stakeholder analysis is to produce a list of stakeholders that might influence the outcome of the project. Once the list of stakeholders is produced, each stakeholder is assessed according to his/her power and interest. In this regard, power is the stakeholder's ability to affect various aspects of the project, either positively or negatively, and interest is defined as the level of concern the stakeholder has with the project. Both the power and interest of the stakeholders are assessed in respect to the task, activity, project, and even toward a specific project objective.

The widely used two axes power and interest grid has four quadrants:

1. high power, high interest stakeholders;
2. high power, low interest stakeholders;
3. low power, high interest stakeholders; and
4. low power low interest stakeholders.

Experience shows that project managers and teams who do use this tool perform the analysis only once at the start of the project and don't revisit the analysis later on. This undermines the value that can be realized using the tool.

Actually, stakeholder analysis is an ongoing task that should be performed on a monthly basis in order to increase the opportunities to influence stakeholders. What's more, throughout the project, new stakeholders become relevant while stakeholders who were part of earlier analysis might become irrelevant. The analysis of power and interest is also an input for communication planning.

Each quadrant in the stakeholders' assessment grid has a directive explaining how to manage the stakeholders within the specific quadrant. The general guidelines for each quadrant are:

1. high power, high interest stakeholders: manage closely;

2. high power, low interest stakeholders: keep satisfied;
3. low power, high interest stakeholders: keep informed; and
4. low, power low interest stakeholders: monitor with minimal effort.

The project team needs to detail further each general guideline into specific communication tasks and activities. The guidelines differ among different teams and different projects. Note that the direction to closely manage stakeholders in the first quadrant relates not only to the extent of communication activities performed, but also to the intensity of the process itself.

Stakeholders who are managed closely are also queried often on how much communication they would prefer. Thus, it might happen that some stakeholders in this group receive fewer reports and updates compared with members in the keep-informed quadrant because they opted to receive less information.

Thinking alert:
Manage closely, similar to the other communication guidelines in the grid, doesn't imply that stakeholders receive more bits of information; rather, it indicates that the stakeholders are allowed a customized communication approach compared with stakeholders in other quadrants. power.

The Power and Interest Grid

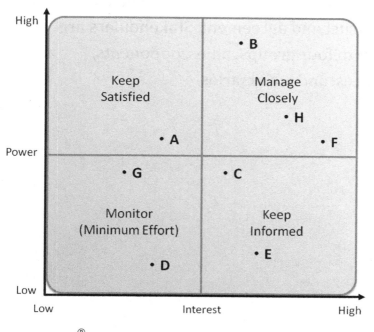

PMBOK® Guide – Fourth Edition, p. 249

Happy Bears

The Power and Interest Grid depicted above, while useful in the context of creating a general understanding of stakeholders support, lacks a more in-depth view of the actual relationships and forecasted behaviors of the stakeholders toward the specific effort.

To understand these better, an alternative view on the analysis of stakeholders is suggested. In this view, stakeholders are analyzed based on their perceived support, implicit or explicit. A four-quadrant grid is likewise employed with two axes as seen below. The axes are trust and agreement. Stakeholders are divided into four groups: allies, opponents, accomplices, and adversaries.

The Trust and Agreement Grid

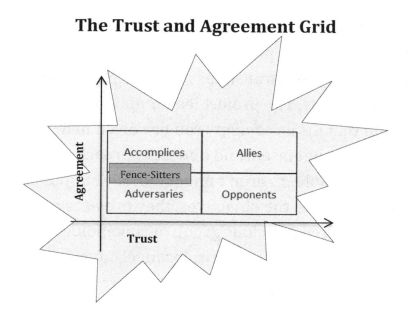

Stakeholders in the **Allies** quadrant are the advocates of the project, having both trust in the project team and agreement with the objectives and the approach used to manage the project. They are supporting unequivocally and will provide assistance when required, help when needed, and advice when requested (sometimes even when it's not requested).

Stakeholders in the **Opponents** quadrant are openly and objectively criticizing elements of the project. They are, to a degree, not in agreement with some objectives of the project and might be questioning the methods employed by the team to achieve the objectives. Nonetheless, there is mutual trust between the project team and these stakeholders that translates into "fair play" in solving disagreements. The project leader and the team are certain that disagreements can be solved in a reasonable, unbiased, and honest approach. While these stakeholders aren't unequivocally supporting the process and the objectives, they prove to be a much required judicious group of stakeholders who can objectively challenge project decisions.

Stakeholders in the **Accomplices** quadrant are outwardly accepting and collaborating with the project team in the process and supportive of the objective. These stakeholders are also said to be giving lip service. It might seem that they agree, but because there is little trust between the project team and these stakeholders, the continued support isn't taken for granted. The project leader and the team can't depend on the support displayed by this stakeholder group because it can easily be substituted by sharp defiance as soon as the environment changes or as soon as the project team is out of hearing range. This makes the accomplices group of stakeholders quite dangerous. Project teams and managers are advised to build trust with these stakeholders. The influence techniques in this guide can be employed to establish trust, specifically the strategy of *Liking* mentioned later in this chapter.

Stakeholders in the **Adversaries** quadrant are un-accepting and not collaborating with the project team in the process and are in disagreement with the objective. An evolving conflict is building between the project team and this group of stakeholders. The project leader and the team can't depend on receiving support from this group, which tends to employ manipulative means to propagate disagreement. Naturally, the group of adversary stakeholders is the most difficult to influence and lead. Theoretically, project team and manager can invest time and effort to build trust and agreement with these stakeholders. Practically, these might be wasted efforts, leading to the opposite result (see more below). After all, people—project teams and managers included—invest too much effort in persuading and convincing the adversary stakeholder group with little valuable results. The focus on this group develops into an openly hostile conflict that resonates with the other stakeholder groups and can create a landslide in the overall level of support.

Reflect on the trust an agreement grid – at work – who are your allies, your opponents, your accomplices, and your adversaries?

Be a Practical Bear

Our behavior of increased focus on the adversary group is quite human and evident in many similar interactions. Imagine a teacher in a classroom where, among 30 pupils, three are in distrust and conflict with the teacher. In most cases, more than half of the teacher's attention will be given to these pupils at the expense of the others. Obviously, the teacher needs to create an environment that supports learning in the class, but the focus on those disturbing the class is counterproductive because it provides opposite results.

So, why do we focus on the adversary group? Psychologically speaking, we have a need to be accepted and loved (or at least liked), and we find it extremely difficult to be in a position where people are un-accepting of us. We go to great lengths to receive appreciation and support from groups of people who disagree with us and/or our goals.

Take a minute to reflect on your efforts in gaining *liking* and appreciation from everyone and investing great efforts to please those who are in hostile conflict and distrusting disagreement at the expense of investing your time building positive relationships with other more supportive individuals.

Letting go of our explicit need for unanimous all-encompassing acceptance isn't an easy task and requires a mental and cognitive shift in how we perceive ourselves and our interactions with the environment in which we operate. Achieving this improved psychological condition enables us to move away from focusing on those who aren't accepting us and instead investing time and effort in those who are supportive or those who haven't made up their mind yet (more on that later).

In the teacher example above, the class, the teacher, and the learning environment would benefit greatly from focus on the main group of pupils who are sitting on the fence, so to speak, waiting to see how the conflict between the teacher and the adversary pupils plays out before deciding which side to choose.

Notwithstanding the two models for stakeholder analysis presented so far, at the outset of each stakeholder interaction, such as a kickoff meeting, a conference call, a town hall meeting, or similar gathering, there are three main attitudes apparent. These attitudes are easily observed by reading body language, words used, and tone of voice. Roughly speaking, there are stakeholders who immediately support, those who oppose, and a larger group of people who are "sitting on the fence." Stakeholders who are fence sitters are waiting to see how things play out. They haven't decided yet whom to support and are making up their minds.

Remember as a general rule of thumb, in any interaction that you might have, approximately 5% of the stakeholders will be against, 5% of the stakeholders will be in favor, and the remaining 90% of stakeholders will be either fence sitters or paying some amount of lip service.

As detailed above, placing emphasis and overt focus on those in opposition is a fatal mistake in building your support coalition and your informal power base. It is also the **most common** mistake.

> **Thinking alert:**
> Often, when building a support coalition, you will place too much emphasis on the stakeholders who are opposed, which will lead to a failed effort.

In an analogy to the teacher example, imagine you are giving a presentation to 100 participants. The presentation is about some change project in marketing that will greatly affect the manufacturing, maintenance, operations, IT, engineering, and sales departments. This is a high profile project with many interests. You are holding a formal kickoff presentation and it is vital that you gain support for this endeavor.

As explained above, about five to ten participants will be totally in favor of your approach and about five to ten participants will be totally against whatever you propose. The remaining participants have not made up their minds yet. This presentation is your opportunity to build a coalition and to influence the stakeholder community to support the project as you move forward.

Most presenters will aim their influence efforts at those opposing, sometimes engaging in verbal confrontations with them during and after the presentation. This is folly because they are unlikely to gain much by arguing with this stakeholder group. The byproduct of discussing the merits with them is that some "fence sitters" will actually join the group of naysayers. This common outcome mirrors the human tendency to side with the underdog—in this case, if you are leading the presentation and have the stage, the underdog will be the blockers.

What you want to do is to speak partly to the supporters and partly to the fence sitters. You wish to create an explicit path of trust for those sitting on the fence to become supporters.

Tip: You can easily recognize those supporting, those against, and the fence sitters. As a rule of thumb, those who are supporting will be sitting in the front rows and those opposing and blocking will be in the back rows.

When is a Bear Not a Bear?

We tend to think that others think in the same way we do. This makes sense because our personal thinking process is the only one we know. Philosophically, we actually can't be certain that others are experiencing events anywhere near the way we do.

The axiomatic assertion concerning colors is a good example because my experience of yellow is probably different compared to others' experience of the color yellow, and I can't relay this experience in any concrete way. I assume that when I say a certain color is yellow, others perceive the same emotional range, cognitive experience, and mental state that I do. It is human to assume that others are experiencing the environment the same way that we do, but it leads to obvious communication challenges.

When interacting with stakeholders, the fallacy that others are viewing situations, scenarios, and the environment as we do is detrimental. Working with stakeholders—assuming that their perception of a certain situation is identical to ours—is at the basis of many failures to influence. Being able to move away from our perception of the situation, which is based on our emotional, mental, and cognitive states, is crucial in gaining the support of others.

Concepts, such as active listening, empathizing, and WIIFM (what is in it for me?) spring to mind; these are actually the techniques that assist us in moving away from our perceptions and in becoming more capable of identifying the perceptions of others.

More about Perception and Communications

Widely held communication models depict two equal participants in communication: the sender and receiver. The Shannon-Weaver Model is a relevant example.

The Shannon-Weaver Communication Model

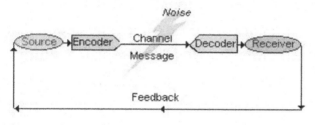

Shannon-Weaver Model

In 1947, Shannon and Weaver suggested a model to describe communication between computer systems. The model can be used to depict TCP/IP (transmission control protocol/Internet protocol Internet communication). In the model is a communication source, an encoder for encoding the message, a channel through which the message flows, a decoder of the message, and the receiver.

The receiver sends feedback of message reception. In the communication channel, there can be interference and noise, e.g., the dropping of IP packets in an ADSL line.

The model was adopted to illustrate interpersonal communication. In workshops, I often joke that psychologists have science envy and borrowing on scientific models and concepts explains elements of human behavior. This is the case with the adoption of the Shannon-Weaver Model into interpersonal communications; it doesn't explain the causes for miscommunication. Social sciences practitioners added elements to the original model to illustrate perceptions that interfere with the message, but the fundamental application of the IT model to interpersonal communication is flawed.

Communication between humans, in contrast to machines, is not linear and balanced; rather, it is haphazard, contingent, context-based, and associative. In order to understand how humans communicate, we need to understand how children develop the spoken language.

One of the pioneers in the research of language and cognitive development is Piaget, a Swiss psychologist and philosopher known for his epistemological studies with children. Piaget demonstrated that children learn words through a bottom-up approach, in contrast to the belief of a top-down mechanism. Children impart a meaning to an object by processing many encounters of different versions of that object.

For example, most individuals globally have a similar understanding of a table. When asked to draw a table, most would use the conceptual model and draw something similar to the drawing below

Cognitive Model of: Table

However, this is just a two-dimensional drawing of lines connected to a parallelogram. How is it that we consider the drawing to represent a table?

Piaget would say that, as children, we saw many examples of tables, probably none that resembled the one in the drawing above. Each time we saw a table, the people around us would say a mostly unintelligible (as we were only babies) sentence that included the word "table." After several hundreds of such occurrences, the word stuck, and we were able to build a lasting image of the **essence of the functionality** of a table. Almost like magic, the conceptual model of a table, as presented above in the drawing, materializes for the word "table."

> **Thinking alert:**
> Every one of us builds a conceptual dictionary based on individual experiences. While the model might appear similar, especially for concrete objects, the meanings that we allocate to the model can be vastly different. As a result, while the Shannon-Weaver Model assumes that people's mental models for words and concepts are identical, they actually aren't. **Communication based on the assumption that two stakeholders mean the same thing when they say a certain word is doomed to fail.** Although we have the same mental model for a table (the cover and the four lines), the **context and associations** that we have for the concept are vastly **different**

When I say "bear," the immediate picture that springs to my mind is my Alaskan encounter with a grizzly. What is your mental image when you hear the word "bear"? What is your mental image when you hear the word "project"? How about rapport, liking, PMO, leadership, influence?

The more abstract the concept, the larger the variation in associated connotations. Communication is hardly an orderly Shannon-Weaver Model; rather, it is more of a tornado of context spiraling down, and the base of the tornado is where mutual understanding is achieved. Our ability to understand each other is based on investigating the associations and context more than the message itself.

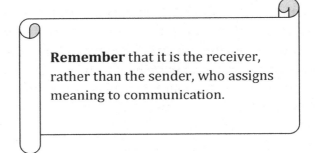

> **Remember** that it is the receiver, rather than the sender, who assigns meaning to communication.

Project managers assume that stakeholders understand what they communicate in words, but actually, the stakeholders decide what to glean from a message based on the context and the associations. In order to validate the intention, the prudent project manager should spend time understanding the meanings that the stakeholders assign to the words, sentences, reports, presentations, etc.

Communication Inferences Tornado

Case Study Example

The following case study exemplifies how comprehending perception divergences is crucial. Without understanding the different perceptions, leading the bears of the matrix organization is doomed to fail.

The case study presents a global telecommunication company that sells to original equipment manufacturers (OEMs), developing both hardware and software. Software development is performed using an Agile project management approach, specifically Scrum processes.

The corporate offices in North America have mandated the inception of a PMO that will globally manage the company's portfolio. Tom Jenkins, a senior project manager, has been appointed head PMO and has recruited three junior employees from various departments with up to three years of work experience.

The company has 80 project managers distributed across 15 sites: seven in North America, four in Europe, and four in Asia and Australia. Some of these project managers are handling marketing projects, others work in integrating new project into operations, and the majority of project managers operate in development. The project managers report to their relevant business units.

Tom is traveling on a business trip to South America; he is meeting with clients to discuss specific aspects of procurement of electronic hardware components. Accompanying him are the VP of marketing, the VP of supply chain, and the VP of customer support. They decide to present the client with several options for product consignment. They prepare a presentation to solve some challenges regarding supply chain and costs of products. The presentation is impeccable and includes several options to resolve the challenges they have been facing with this particular client. They perceive that by addressing these issues up front, they will be able to move forward and increase sales with the client.

Halfway through the presentation, however, the client cuts them short. He considers the problem a trust issue and, therefore, changing the consignment and product costs will not resolve it. The client is troubled and agitated that Tom and his team are not viewing this as a trust issue, and he decides to cancel the remaining meetings to consult with his managers. Tom and his colleagues are surprised with the behavior of the client, but because the client is adamant in his refusal, they head back to the home office.

Perception of issues is crucial in creating, developing, and building personal influencing power. The ability to influence without authority is based on one's capacity to view an issue from more than one perspective and preferably from the perspective of the other side as well. This is known as empathy (not to be confused with sympathy). Understanding that an issue has many dimensions and is perceived differently by various stakeholders not only prevents misunderstandings, but also increases and provides opportunities for creative results.

Making the Bear Like You

In *The Psychology of Persuasion*, acclaimed persuasion expert Robert Cialdini describes six persuasion techniques that are often employed manipulatively by marketers and sellers to lure us into purchasing items we do not intend to buy.

Methods, such as the foot in the door (which is based on the social stipulation of reciprocation), are extremely powerful in guiding us to action. Of the six techniques, liking, as an influence approach, is probably one of the least used and least manipulative in a business setting.

Liking, therefore, has many advantages as an influencing tool and is described below. It is up to you, the reader, to decide whether to use it and, if so, when, how, and to what extent. In any case, liking is a powerful way to create informal power in project teams without much effort. (It resembles, to an extent, sympathy.)

Liking is the creation and development of feelings of identification, bonding, and rapport through which one can obtain informal power and can influence an individual or a party to commit to a certain course of action.

Liking has many facets and can be achieved through the following categorical approaches:

1. Similar outward appearances can help instill liking.
2. Mutual beliefs, lifestyles, and/or religion create a strong liking between individuals.
3. Similar backgrounds promote liking. For example, participants sitting at the same table in workshops immediately find a common background, e.g., the school they attended, hobbies they share, a good book they've read, etc.
4. Positive acknowledgment, feedback, and outright compliments and flattery can go a long way in creating liking; they might not be considered honorable, but they are powerful.
5. Interaction, cooperation, and collaboration, i.e., mutual work, tend to create liking when the experience is positive and successful.

Liking based on any of the five mentioned categories is effective and enables the initiator to create a strong bond with individuals and groups.

However, liking is usually shunned as an influence strategy. It is easy to remember how those pupils who interacted with the teachers were usually mocked and called "teacher's pets," "bootlickers," and brownnosers.

Because people tend to avoid using these tools, the opposite result can occur, i.e., in most organizations, hardly any acknowledgement is given and hardly any liking is developed. Simple thank you cards and emails are neglected and appreciation on the personal level is often avoided.

Within this atmosphere, a minimal use of liking as an influence strategy can go a long way. It provides informal power and the ability to influence and create coalitions of supporters. That is not to say that liking should be used haphazardly and without consideration; rather, the idea is that genuine liking— using any of the approaches mentioned above— should be pursued.

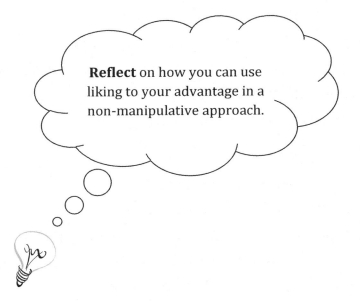

Reflect on how you can use liking to your advantage in a non-manipulative approach.

Virtual teams that operate in the global environment are often devoid of any liking whatsoever. Small efforts go a long way in the virtual sphere. While I recommend investing time to create bonding between the stakeholders in my soft skills workshop, the opposite usually occurs.

We treat others as resources, which if you think about, is quite demeaning. How is it that we stopped calling others "people" and instead refer to them as "resources" who must deliver work results? The typical status reporting conference call has no schmoozing time allocated. Rather, it is a round-robin exchange where the meeting manager requests participants to report their achievements.

We don't even consider investing time in building rapport and liking in virtual settings. These can be incorporated easily into the virtual meeting by allocating a few minutes for small talk. Other methods to increase rapport and build liking can include:

- asking meeting participants to share a personal anecdote about themselves;
- asking meeting participants to share a picture of themselves engaging in a hobby;
- asking meeting participants to share information about their culture or location's specifics, such as a holiday, customs, cultural aspects, etc.;
- creating a shared social site where team members can interact informally (this can also be achieved by creating a closed group on LinkedIn or Facebook); and
- playing a virtual game with fun prizes to increase informal interaction.

Each of the above methods increases liking because it builds interaction, cooperation, and collaboration. As mentioned above, the virtual environment in most organizations is often devoid of any interpersonal interaction, so a small investment in building liking can go a long way.

Remember
to project influence and leadership

1. Manage stakeholders by identifying them and analyzing their interest and power;
2. Use the identification as the basis for communication planning, or assess stakeholders according to their trust and agreement (i.e., allies, opponents, accomplices, and adversaries);
3. Construct a method to lead the stakeholders who are sitting on the fence;
4. Avoid giving too much emphasis to the adversaries;
5. Accept that stakeholders will have different perceptions of the same issues; strive to learn these perceptions through active listening and questioning; and
6. Consider using *liking* to increase your influence without authority power.

More Thinking: Did You Know?

Effective leaders focus on the circle of influence rather than on the circle of concern, as described in Covey's *The Seven Habits of Highly Effective People.* This directly contrasts others who focus on the circle of concern. In relation to project management, and specifically change control process, a project manager and team that focuses on the circle of concern often communicates what they can't achieve because they haven't been given something.

Effective project managers and teams would rather describe what they can achieve with what they have or with what can be given to them. There is a big difference between the two options- next time focus on the circle of influence.

Circle Of Influence and Concern

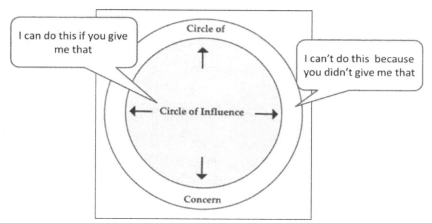

CHAPTER
FOUR

**Important-
the Leadership Bear**

Important-
the Leadership Bear

In her lovely book, *Bear Snores on*, author Karma Wilson describes our friend the bear asleep during his winter hibernation period. This time, a group of annoying critters invades the privacy of his cave and use it for their personal needs. They prepare food, pop some popcorn, light a fire, dance, and have an effervescent good time.

Unknowingly they are depriving the bear of his much-needed winter sleep. When at long last, the bear awakens, the small forest animals scurry away only to find the bear, instead of wholeheartedly devouring them, complaining that they did not share in their fun. In order to placate the bear, the animals prepare more food for him, and when he is finished eating, he tells his guests a bear story, and they become tired after a night of debauchery and fall asleep.

In this story, the bear is displaying two situational leadership approaches: After being woken rather rudely by the unwanted guests, the bear assesses his options. Realizing that the miniature scale of his uninvited guests would not provide sufficient nourishment, he moves to facilitating style from the coercive leadership style. Thus, he influences his friends to prepare more food for him so he can eat as well.

This chapter introduces the concept of situational leadership within the framework of active listening and empathy as a means to acquire informal power.

Four Bear Types – Situational Leadership

Over the years, many leadership theories have emerged. In the past, great man and trait theories prevailed. These contended, as the name implies, that leaders are either born or have a certain set of defined characteristics in order to become leaders. The challenge of these theories is that they fail to explain typical occurrences in the modern organization.

Consider, for example, the department manager who displays remarkable leadership aptitude, gaining the appreciation of both the people in the department and of management. Then, he receives a promotion and moves to lead a bigger department in another part of the organization. Suddenly, he falters, his reports shun him, complaining that he is a dictator; his peers perceive him as obnoxious and his results are mediocre. This eventuality can't be explained using the great man or trait theories. According to these, a leader will remain successful regardless of the external environment.

Contemporary approaches in leadership have abandoned the concepts that leadership is an inborn trait or a specific and certain predefined set of skills and competencies. Rather, the concept of situational leadership has emerged and two theories have been proposed. Situational leadership articulates that effective leaders are able to change their style according to the situation. Most of the leadership styles that have been identified within these two situational leadership theories require a developed proficiency in **empathy, active listening, and the ability to understand complex human and team interactions**, coinciding with the global human resource research detailed below.

We describe two situational leadership theories: Blanchard and Heresy's four leadership styles, and later, Daniel Goleman's six leadership styles. Both models claim that the successful leader is able to easily change his style according to the situation he encounters. This requires developed soft skills.

Interestingly enough, non-related global research performed by human resource organizations analyzed dimensions of leadership characteristics. The research indicated approximately 20 characteristics found in leaders of global businesses. Among the characteristics are fairness, humility, trust, conflict resolution, vision, political savvy, openness, integrity, creativity, assertiveness, persistence, consistency, commitment, delegating ability, creation of reality, humorous, active listening, and effective communication skills.

When further elaborated and analyzed, many of the characteristics are related to the same proficiencies mentioned in the situational leadership theories.

The first situational leadership theory we discuss is the Blanchard and Heresy model, which defines both the level of maturity of the team and the explicit leadership style applicable to the specific maturity level. The model outlines the situational leadership grid, consisting of two axes: the directive behavior axis and the supportive behavior axis. **Directive behavior is clearly telling people what do**, where and when and how to do it, while also closely supervising their performance. **Supportive behavior is listening, providing support and encouragement, and facilitating involvement**.

The Heresy and Blanchard model

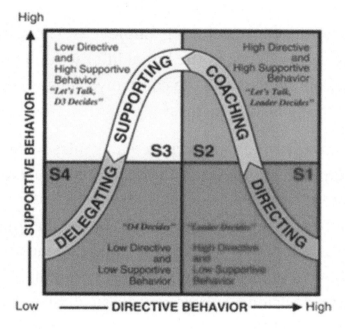

S1 quadrant characterizes teams who are missing the initial direction and expertise. The leadership style relevant for this situation is defined as "directing." The leader instructs the team, giving his vision and direction to the team. These teams are often newly formed, consisting of novice members unable to perform and yet do not take responsibility for performing. The leader instructs the team, defines roles and responsibilities, and assigns activities and tasks. Failing to recognize this situation might lead to the demoralization of the new employees and missed opportunities for developing employees. These might be long-term effects, as the initial interaction between the new employees and the company is negative, creating long lasting distrust.

S2 quadrant characterizes teams missing both the required expertise and the relationship between team members. The leadership style relevant for this situation is defined as "coaching." The leader supports the team in building the relationship and teaches them how to gain the required information in order to make the decisions. Subsequent to the deliberations, the leader decides. Leaders who fail to recognize this situation might leave too much decision space for the team, or alternatively, they might fail to coach the team in the decision-making process.

S3 quadrant characterizes teams who have the necessary skill-set but are lacking in relationships. The leadership style relevant tor this situation is defined as "supporting." The leader promotes team decision making, providing the required support in managing the interpersonal interactions. Typical for

Proper training and assimilation of new styles also require support from the environment, initially in a workshop setting and then through a member of the organization. The benefit is an increased toolbox in handling the various situations, translating to better business results.

The Six Bear Types – Situational Leadership

In the article "Leadership that gets results," Daniel Goleman, who coined the term "emotional intelligence," presents six situational leadership styles, each one originating from different components of emotional intelligence, capabilities, and competencies. Each of the leadership styles has a specific impact on the working environment of the business and its overall performance.

Goleman describes the specific business environment that each style satisfies. He asserts that most individuals prefer one or two styles and find it difficult to assume other styles. He explains that potent leaders are able to move gracefully from style to style, selecting the appropriate style much like a skilled golf player decides on the appropriate golf club for the situation. Expanding a style repertoire enables leaders to handle more situations. Goleman further asserts that each style is applicable and useful in an appropriate scenario.

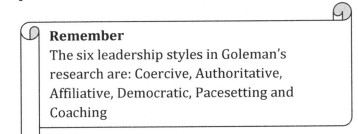

Remember
The six leadership styles in Goleman's research are: Coercive, Authoritative, Affiliative, Democratic, Pacesetting and Coaching

We detail each of the styles below as well as insights concerning them.

Coercive leaders: Paraphrasing, they are the "angry bear" type. They demand immediate and complete compliance. They dictate, define roles and responsibilities, use punishment, and to an extent instill fear in the organization. Their motto is, "My way or the highway." This leadership style can be described in a few words: "Do what I tell you to do."

Is the coercive leadership style always inappropriate in the modern organization? Not necessarily. There are times when significant and tough decisions have to be made quickly, and postponing the decisions can have grave results; the coercive style can be useful in these circumstances.

Authoritative leaders: Paraphrasing, they are the "mother bear" type. They help guide people toward a common vision, and they set objectives and define the end goal. This leadership style can be described in a few words as, "Come with me."

Is the authoritative style always appropriate? Reading the article, it might seem so because this style has the highest positive impact on overall organizational environment. Based on business experience, however, **there are situations in which this leadership style can be seen as disturbing and pompous**. Consider the team of experts that are self-guiding and familiar with the objectives—an authoritative leader will get in the way of this team and hinder their performance.

Affiliative leaders: Paraphrasing, they are the "romping bear" type. They maintain harmony, create relationships, foster relationships, and in general, maintain the emotional bonds. This leadership style can be described in a few words as "**People come first**." When the team has been undergoing emotional strain or when the team spirit has been negatively impacted by organizational changes, this leadership style is appropriate.

Is the affiliative style always appropriate? The affiliative leader emphasizes feeling, support, and team spirit at the expense of performance because team spirit comes first. Having too much of this style can lead to mediocre business results.

Democratic leaders: Paraphrasing, they are the "salmon-catching bear" type. They work in a team and build consensus through participative collaboration. This leadership style can be described in a few words as, "**What do you think**?" The democratic decision-making process is paramount for this leadership style. This is a very popular style in many west European countries and especially in Sweden.

Is the democratic style always appropriate? Too much of this style can **lead to time wasted on endless meetings and deliberations without results**. In addition, this style can lead to negative team decision processes and results, such as Groupthink or the so-called "wisdom" of the crowd decision making. What if the crowd is stupid?

Pacesetting leaders: Paraphrasing, they are the "footprints in the sand bear" type. They expect superb performance and excellence achieved through demanding self-direction. This leadership style can be described in a few words as, "**Do as I do—now!**"

At face value, this seems like a powerful leadership style to employ, but it negatively affects most environments. The pacesetter requires complete compliance with his way of working, which stifles creativity and free thinking. Granted, he is a top performer and demands of himself as much as he demands of others, but he doesn't tolerate alternate approaches, seeing subversion everywhere and ridding himself of the top achievers so as not to endanger his supremacy.

I have had the regrettable opportunity of viewing a pacesetter while consulting for one of my global clients. He was one of the world's top experts in his field with over 25 years of experience; he commanded an organization of more than 900 employees. In eight years, he was able to instill a reign of fear throughout the organization. All his seven top-performing managers had left—some with tears, being replaced by "yes" managers, i.e., mediocre and submissive. His reputation was across the board, and no high performing manager in the industry was willing to come and work for him.

Coaching leaders: Paraphrasing, these are the "fatherly bear" types. They develop the people for the future and teach how to catch the fish, giving the rod instead of the fish. This leadership style can be described in a few words as, "**Try this.**"

The article asserts that most organizations are failing to embrace more of the coaching style and would actually improve by investing in coaching.

Reflect – what is your dominant style? Coercive, Authoritative, Affiliative, Democratic, Pacesetting, Coaching

Once more, it is apparent that influencing and convincing is situation dependent. Using coercion when the team has just suffered an emotional blow would not be prudent. On the other hand, in a crisis, striving for democratic decision-making is counterproductive. A team that does not have a direction will require a leadership style that is authoritative rather than affiliative.

Effective leaders are able to master more than two leadership styles; they are cognizant of the team or individual needs and are able to easily shift between styles.

Case Study Example

With the assistance of the case study, we'll describe the four maturity levels of Blanchard and Heresy.

Tom is sitting with his three new recruits. All of them have four years of experience in previous roles and companies. They seem eager to start the work and offer ideas. Johanna says that it's best to start immediately working with marketing on the new product. James says that he thinks the problems are with engineering and they should convene a meeting to roll out the new approach for concurrent engineering. Gino says that finance is not operating correctly and the immediate course of action is to investigate deficiencies in the ERP system and map resulting effects.

Tom listens carefully to his team members. Being educated in situational leadership models, he knows what his team requires.

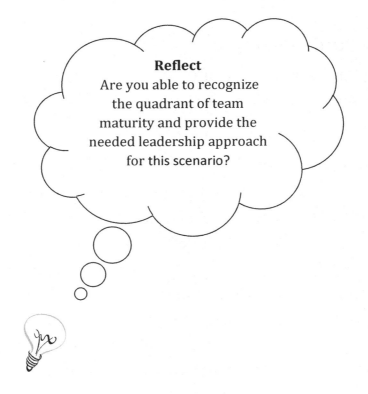

Reflect
Are you able to recognize the quadrant of team maturity and provide the needed leadership approach for this scenario?

The team is exhibiting a medium-level maturity. On one hand, they are eager and willing to work, but on the other hand, they seem somewhat without direction, and their level of performance is relatively low. The appropriate leadership response is coaching, which provides high task focus and high relationship focus. The team can perform the job at least to some extent; they might be a bit overconfident about their ability.

While directing leadership might de-motivate the team and can lead to resistance, but coaching offers constrained and guided freedom. Tom must explain and clarify his suggested course of action and decisions. Tom will spend time listening and advising, helping the team develop the necessary skills to perform well.

Tom discusses Johanna's idea. He asks her and the team what might be other options to handle Johanna's assignments. He emphasizes that while working with marketing on the new product immediately can prove beneficial, marketing might push back against such an upfront assault. He offers to analyze the objective of the activity together during their next team meeting. He suggests that Johanna begins with initial data gathering about the specific stakeholder groups in marketing and their perceived future support.

Next, he asks James about the challenges apparent in the engineering department. He recommends that the first step might be a root cause analysis with a small team, rather than convening the entire engineering team, which might result in forceful opposition.

Finally, he invites Gino to provide further information regarding the deficiencies in the ERP system and adds that investigation and mapping is a good idea. He proposes that the mapping will be their first topic to discuss in the next team meeting.

Tom then congratulates the team for their motivation and willingness to learn and to improve the organization. He expresses his confidence in their abilities to succeed in bringing change in the various activities that they are leading.

Notice how Tom is practicing the leadership style, inviting collaboration, creating rapport and yet making the decision himself—that is exactly the approach required to influence and lead this situation.

Applying the Chapter's Concepts

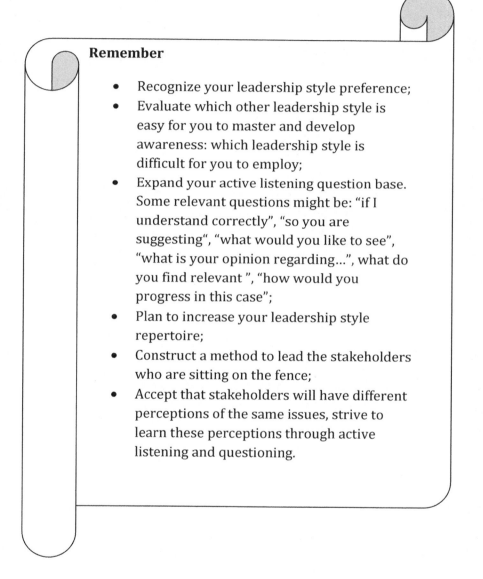

Remember

- Recognize your leadership style preference;
- Evaluate which other leadership style is easy for you to master and develop awareness: which leadership style is difficult for you to employ;
- Expand your active listening question base. Some relevant questions might be: "if I understand correctly", "so you are suggesting", "what would you like to see", "what is your opinion regarding...", what do you find relevant ", "how would you progress in this case";
- Plan to increase your leadership style repertoire;
- Construct a method to lead the stakeholders who are sitting on the fence;
- Accept that stakeholders will have different perceptions of the same issues, strive to learn these perceptions through active listening and questioning.

CHAPTER
FIVE

Special-
the Elevator Bear

Special-
the Elevator Bear

Are you familiar with the elevator pitch? I'm sure you've heard about it. There are some variations to it, but by and large the question is, "What would you tell the CEO of a very successful Fortune 500 company [say, the late-Steve Jobs] if you were to meet him by chance on an elevator ride in a high-rise business building?"

The elevator pitch revolves around the notion that we are, to an extent, salespeople in our jobs and in the companies where we work. When required to deliver a message—specifically, while presenting to senior management—we should be able to do so briefly, concisely, engagingly, and within 30 seconds.

There has been much change since the original appearance of the elevator pitch concept some 60 years ago. Lately there have been those who questioned the entire idea. Yet, various elements endure and are relevant today, e.g., the need to package the message in alignment with the specific stakeholder.

The only reason we communicate is to pass on information that in some way supports our point of view, understanding, values, beliefs, expectations, and hoping/assuming that the recipient will act on the message.

We have already mentioned that many times we are failing to communicate our message because the recipient is focusing on everything but our message. In order to increase our success in relaying our message, we should keep the end of the communication interaction in mind. With emails, for example, we all know that people are bombarded by them; thus, it is counterproductive to send long emails with obscure subject lines without explicitly defining the required outcome.

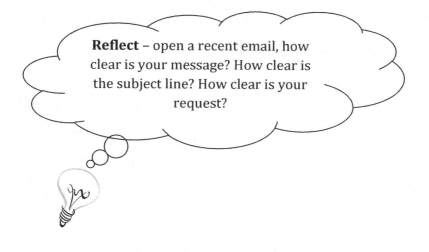

Reflect – open a recent email, how clear is your message? How clear is the subject line? How clear is your request?

An email and any other written messaging tool should always start with the purpose and the required action upfront. A long email might begin with a brief summary of the subject and the subject's contents. All other information, such as relevant attachments, specific details, and intermediate findings, should be below the purpose and the action required. The subject line of the email must concisely summarize either the objective or the action required.

Oral and verbal communication under time constraints for busy stakeholders should, to an extent, follow the concept of the elevator pitch. However, elevators today are much faster and the ride hardly lasts 30 seconds—at most, all you have is 10 seconds to influence a stakeholder toward a specific course of action. In addition, stakeholders are not necessarily senior executives riding by chance with you in a once in a lifetime opportunity.

Rather, all stakeholders are busy, stressed for time, and unfortunately, generally impatient. *Like it or not, messages in the modern age are become even shorter, attention spans are fleeting, and time is measured in minutes and seconds.*

It is beyond the scope of this book to discuss and judge the philosophical aspect of this phenomenon and the impact it has on our lives, but I wish to impart to you the practical guideline: **A ten-second attention grabber followed by relevant information, a concise message, an example for the wanted course of action, and a request to follow through is the appropriate structure for messages in today's global business.**

For example: Tom, the PMO manager, is publishing a company newsletter. He wants to make sure that people are using the newly implemented human resource system for blocking out vacation time in their resource calendars.

*So far, the level of accuracy of resource calendars has been less than adequate, affecting the ability to correctly forecast future project load in portfolio planning. Tom and his team decided to address the issue in the upcoming electronic version of the newsletter. Following the guidelines for written messages structure: **Attention, Relevant Information, Message, Example, and Do, also known as the ARMED acronym,** they've composed the following message:*

Bali, Seychelles, Greenland—these beautiful islands are waiting for you. Are you planning a vacation? The new human resource system is there for you to update your vacation time. Make sure you do that, so we can plan ahead and so you don't receive numerous emails and messages on your vacation demanding immediate response. For example, I just recently traveled to Australia. I updated the system, but the question remains: Is Australia an island?

Please update your vacation time now on our company site @.....

While the above message might seem quite ludicrous, it does the job. Remember **ARMED**.

Ultimately—Black, Grizzly, and Polar Bears

There is an extremely useful influencing model that assists in directing a message and increasing the influence spectrum and the ability to convince. The model discusses four individual communication styles and maps them on a 2x2 matrix, as seen below:

Responsive and Directive Grid

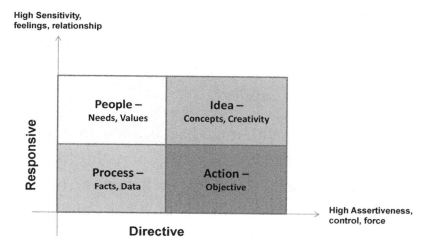

The two axes are assertiveness and responsiveness. *Assertiveness* **is the level of force, control, and directness of behavior**. High assertive individuals tend to push their ideas at the expense of others, be more forceful and directive, and make decisions quickly while exposing themselves to higher risk. ***Responsiveness* is the level of sensitivity, willingness to share emotions and feelings, and concern about relationships**. High responsive individuals tend to show sensitivity, emphasize sharing of emotions and display of feelings, and would prefer maintaining relationships to task completion.

In the article, "Revisiting Communication: A 'New Way' To Manage It" by Prof. Pierre Casse from 1994, the four-communication-style model is presented along with a questionnaire assisting in identifying individual preferred style.

When working with models, it is important to remember that they are an abstract of reality. A model's purpose is to clarify and help analyze by removing unnecessary information. I noticed that some people give too much focus to the model instead of looking at the process itself. **Make sure you balance between the model and reality and avoid tagging people for an eternity**. The four communication styles model helps in analyzing preferences for communication and will vastly increase your influence; make sure you re-examine your analysis regularly. Also, communication preferences imply that an individual chooses a certain style and can also switch to other styles if supported and coached—nothing is set in stone.

Now, that I have warned you enough, here are the four styles that will greatly affect your influence:

1. process communication style;
2. people communication style;
3. action communication style; and
4. idea communication style.

Process communication style is on the *low responsive and low assertive* scale. It is also known as the thinker or the analyzer communication style in similar models. Individuals who are process oriented tend to be systematic, logical, factual, verbose, unemotional, cautious, and patient.

The style is grounded in the scientific method and the search for the correct answer is more important than the speed of the decision. These individuals will discuss facts, procedures, planning, organizing, controlling, and testing. They will emphasize testing, analyzing, observing, and proving through examination. They will be found in the quality, finance, engineering, and manufacturing departments.

We'll find process style individuals also in large public-sector organizations where rules and procedures are highly important and determine how decisions are made.

Thinking alert:
It is not that individuals working in these environments are naturally process oriented; rather, process oriented individuals tend to be drawn or migrate to these environments.

Process style tends to be ridiculed in the media and in modern business where the focus is on next quarter financial results. Effective process-oriented individuals can reduce risks, optimize results, and create an environment of improvements based on data. Poorly used, it leads to analysis paralysis: too much debating and hardly any decision making.

When the proposing and reasoning style characteristics aren't balanced, the solution isn't achieved. The famous situation where a committee decides to sanction another committee to look into the analysis is all too common.

People communication style is on the *high responsive and low assertive* scale. It is also known as the relater or the supporter communication style in similar models. Individuals who are people oriented tend to be spontaneous, empathetic, warm, subjective, emotional, perceptive, and sensitive.

This style is founded on the concept that the best leaders want to bring value by listening to others and doing what provides the greater good for all. Individuals will discuss people, needs, motivations, teamwork, communications, feelings, team spirit, and understanding. They will emphasize self-development, sensitivity, awareness, cooperation, beliefs, values, expectations, and relations.

They will be found in human resources, customer care, onsite support, and to an extent marketing departments. They will also be working in care-related occupations, such as nursing, social work, education, etc.

> **Thinking alert:**
> It is not that individuals working in these environments are naturally people oriented; rather, people oriented individuals tend to be drawn or migrate to these environments.

People communication style might lead to an exaggerated participative management approach where individuals feel their contribution is valued. At times, this style might prefer good relations to task completion and promote consensus over meeting objectives. As group cohesiveness is important, the phenomena of "groupthink" might occur because group members are aiming to reduce conflict and reaching consensus without properly analyzing and evaluating ideas and methods.

People style is received with mixed sentiments; while appropriate in some environments, it is out of the question for others. Effective people-oriented individuals can boost team performance, empower individuals to succeed, and create an environment where weaknesses are tolerated, which increases motivation. Poorly used, it leads to mediocre results because people are favored over results.

When the sharing and listening aren't balanced, understanding isn't achieved. The team that keeps on sharing and sharing, never listening to each other, resulting in mismatched perceptions is quite distinct.

Action communication style is on the *low responsive and high assertive* scale. It is also known as the task or the driver-communication style in similar models. Individuals who are action oriented tend to be pragmatic, direct, impatient, decisive, and energetic.

This style is about getting things done through pushing, demanding, and making clear what they want accomplished. These individuals will discuss results, objectives, performance, productivity, efficiency, and moving ahead. They will emphasize responsibility, feedback, experience, challenges, achievements, change, and decisions. They will be found in project management, mid-level management, IT, and manufacturing departments.

Thinking alert:
It is not that individuals working in these environments are naturally action oriented; rather, action-oriented individuals tend to be drawn or migrate to these environments.

Action style might lead to results that are not aligned with business objectives because a mechanism for evaluating activities against goals is not valued, and at times, action style individuals fail to see the big picture over the details. This style can also lead to fatigue within the organization as resources are working without consideration for individuals' needs.

Action style is what many organizations are looking for when recruiting managers and leaders. Effective action-oriented individuals can increase short-term results, get things done, and be extremely efficient. Poorly used, it leads to a cutthroat environment where trust is scarce and coercion rules. When the demanding and exchanging aren't balanced, the deal isn't achieved. The leader who demands without giving, insists on his goals without reciprocating, and isn't willing to let the other side save face exemplifies the shortcomings of this style.

Idea communication style is on the *high responsive and high assertive* scale. It is also known as the expressive or the socialize-communication style in similar models. Individuals who are idea oriented tend to be imaginative, charismatic, complex, egocentric, unrealistic, creative, and provocative.

This style is about looking at the future and opportunities in the future, mobilizing people through moving together toward a certain future. These individuals will discuss concepts, innovation, creativity, opportunities, possibilities, grand designs, and interdependence. They will emphasize alternatives, new ways, new methods, improvement, revolution, potential, and solutions. They will be found in marketing, sales, business development departments, and sometimes in upper management in specific industries.

> **Thinking alert:**
> It is not that individuals working in these environments are naturally idea oriented; rather, idea oriented-individuals tend to be drawn or migrate to these environments.

Idea style is a way to cut through bureaucracy and red tape, bypassing processes and looking at things differently. It is only effective if it can create resonance with others who share these ideals in order to deliver the promised future.

Idea style is usually what people think of when illustrating leadership characteristics. Effective idea-oriented individuals can instill a collaborative environment, inspire others with a vision, and move other toward long-term objectives. Poorly used, it leads to ignored details, especially by those who aren't aligned with the "bigger picture." When the connecting and envisioning aren't balanced, the cooperation is lacking. The leader creates a farfetched vision they are unable to articulate; it is a typical shortcoming.

Let's explore the impacts of this model: Imagine someone from marketing whose communication style is idea, in a meeting, discussing options for product features with a group of quality and finance managers. He will be presenting about creative concepts, the new way to work, and how the company will operate in the future. They, on the other hand, will not be convinced or influenced by his fluffy words. Hence a mismatch in communication occurs.

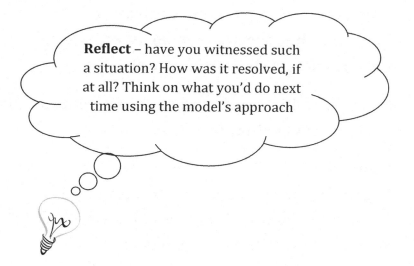

The following are guidelines on how to **influence, convince, and build power with the four communication styles**. Naturally, it is easier if your communication style matches the style of your audience. **Many times, though, you are meeting with colleagues who have other preferred styles.**

For example, let's assume that your preferred communication style is **action**. You are discussing an opportunity with a diverse team whose members have other communication style preferences. In order to influence and convince them to a specific course of action, you should **incorporate and include in your message and approach communication components that are answering all individual communication style requirements**.

In order to influence and convince individuals who are *process* oriented it is important to:

1. Be precise;
2. Organize your presentation in logical order;
3. Breakdown your recommendation to logical steps;
4. Show options with pros and cons;
5. Do not rush the process-oriented individual; and
6. Outline your proposal.

In order to influence and convince individuals who are *people* oriented it is important to:

1. Allow for small talk;
2. Stress the relationship between the proposal and the people concerned;
3. Show how they worked well in the past;
4. Indicate support from well-respected individuals; and

5. Incorporate informality into your discussion and presentation.

In order to influence and convince individuals who are *action* oriented it is important to:

1. Focus on results;
2. State your best recommendation;
3. Be as brief as possible;
4. Emphasize the practicality of your ideas; and
5. Use visual aids.

In order to influence and convince individuals who are *idea* oriented it is important to:

1. Allow enough time for discussion;
2. Do not become impatient when someone is free associating;
3. Be conceptual and discuss the broader view of the topic;
4. Stress uniqueness of the topic at hand; and
5. Emphasize the future state and the value achieved.

It is common in the global environment that a team of individuals will consist of all four communication style preferences. To an extent, their communication requirements will contradict each other and in order to influence and convince you will have to juggle between answering all participants' style preferences. **The Z model is practical to use when communicating in these settings** because it answers all required influence patterns as follows:

The Z Model Communication Scheme

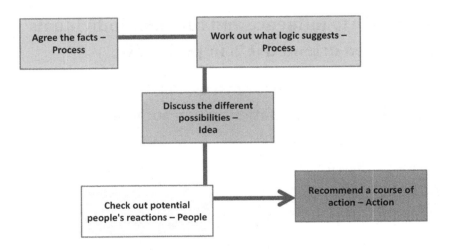

We start by handling **process communication** preference by discussing and agreeing on the facts. We examine and debate the logical course of action, still influencing the process-oriented individuals. We move to the **idea realm**, looking at the big picture possibilities of our suggested course of action. We exchange opinions concerning possible outcomes. Our next base to cover is **people-oriented preference**; we listen actively to potential reactions to the suggested plan, gauging feelings and emotions. We close by detailing the proposal, specifics, responsibilities, and action items, thus answering the **action communication** preferences.

Case Study Example

Over half a year, Lauren prepared an extensive, in-depth, robust updated product life cycle to handle the deficiencies of the current methodology. She based her analysis and solution partially on the requirements from the project and product community. She is ready to present her proposal to the stakeholders, and she understands that receiving support from them is crucial.

Thoroughly educated with the ins and outs of individual communication and influencing preferences, she formulates her presentation on the Z model. She starts the presentation with three slides depicting the current system and its drawbacks, the data received from the stakeholders, and the gap analysis that she performed. She asks for comments from the participants. She moves then to illustrate the model she used for constructing her proposal, offering two alternatives and explaining the reasoning for selecting the specific solution.

These are the first two steps of the Z model geared toward the process-oriented individuals. Her next slide is a top-down view of the product life cycle. She explains the two approaches that she integrated: linear and iterative development. She offers participants the opportunity to deliberate on the long-term possibilities and consequences of the suggested course of action.

Thus, she covers the next step of the Z model: discussing possibilities. Next, Lauren asks for feedback from the participants regarding their perceptions of the suggested change. She listens carefully, taking notes and promising answers when she can't provide them upfront. Because she worked hard beforehand on stakeholder management (remember the second chapter), she receives mostly support and only a few objections. Checking the reactions, she handles the individual with communication preference. Lastly, Lauren moves to the action communication style in the Z model.

Using several slides, she details the short-term rollout plan, including due dates. She specifies the commitment she needs from the participants as well as accountabilities and responsibilities, adding that her team will contact them in the following weeks to further detail the short-term plans. She summarizes by thanking the participants for their time and asks for continued support in the change.

Thinking alert:

While being effective and enabling results, the **Z model is not a mechanical process**; rather, it is an investigation into mutual understanding. **Moving among the steps is an exercise in flow of communication** and not a check box completion procedure. Focusing on the technical aspect of the model will lead to a superficial process that usually fails.

Applying the Chapter's Concepts

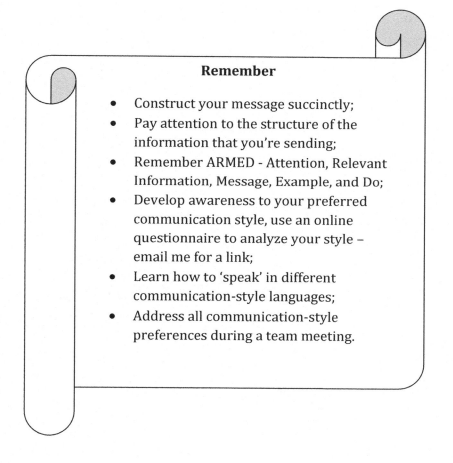

Remember

- Construct your message succinctly;
- Pay attention to the structure of the information that you're sending;
- Remember ARMED - Attention, Relevant Information, Message, Example, and Do;
- Develop awareness to your preferred communication style, use an online questionnaire to analyze your style – email me for a link;
- Learn how to 'speak' in different communication-style languages;
- Address all communication-style preferences during a team meeting.

CHAPTER SIX

Summary

Summary

The book is constructed from big to small. We started with discussing the stakeholder community in general, providing tools and techniques to lead and influence. We moved to leading the team by analyzing situations and changing the approach according to the situation. We concluded with influence targeted toward the individual based on the communication preferences grid and the Z model.

Summarizing the main concepts found in this book with key-points to remember:

1. The first chapter defined key concepts, starting with the matrix organization, moving into influence and leadership and various sources of power.
   a. Where influence is the process, power is the resource.
   b. Learn how to assess and use different types of power.
   c. Bear in mind that, even when you do obtain position-based power, using it is viewed negatively in the modern organization. Alternatively, develop your personal power as

described in this book.

2. The second chapter introduced stakeholders' identification and analysis tools.

   a. Manage stakeholders by listing them and mapping their interest and power; alternatively, assess stakeholders based on trust and agreement.

   b. Using the later analysis, map stakeholders who, at the outset, are sitting on the fence; construct a method to lead them.

   c. Make sure you avoid emphasizing the adversaries; instead, focus on the stakeholders supporting you, and this way you will influence those on the fence.

   d. Accept that stakeholders will have different perceptions of the same issues; strive to learn these perceptions through active listening and questioning.

   e. Consider using strategies for building influence, such as liking.

3. The third chapter discussed leadership styles and their impact on informal power and influence propensity.

   a. Identify your leadership style preference.

b. Evaluate which other leadership style is easy for you to master.

c. Develop awareness into which leadership style is difficult for you to employ; expand your active listening question base.

d. Relevant questions are: "If I understand correctly..." "So you are suggesting..." "What would you like to see?" "What is your opinion regarding..." "What do you find relevant?" "How would you progress in this case?" These and many others assist in developing active listening.

e. Ask colleagues to provide you feedback on your leadership style.

4. The fourth chapter presented the personal communication style preference model and the method to address the various styles.

a. Make your message brief. Pay attention to the structure of the information that you're sending. Remember ARMED.

b. Develop awareness to your preferred communication style, and use an online questionnaire to analyze your style (email me for a link).

c. Learn how to speak in different communication style languages.

d. Use the Z model to address all communication style preferences during a team meeting.

e. Make sure you learn about cultural preferences and their interdependencies to communication styles.

In the beginning of the book, I shared a bear story with you. I hope you don't encounter a bear in the wild because other than verifying its gender and speaking loudly and slowly, there is nothing much to do. However, with the bears in the matrix organization, using the concepts in this book, there are many things you can accomplish. I wish you the best of luck with influencing and leading the denizens of the matrix. In the next pages you will find a summary of how to influence the styles.

Responsive and Directive Grid

High Sensitivity,
Feelings, Relationship

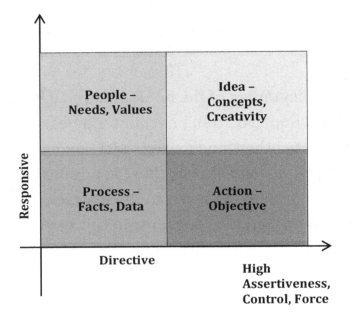

People Style

➢ Energy – moving with, empathetic

➢ Actions – sharing, listening

➢ Outcome – understanding

➢ Key words – people, needs, sensitivity, relationships, beliefs, co-operation, team spirit

➢ Cultures – Asia, Japan, social professions, HR, health and education

Idea Style

➢ Energy – moving together, inspiring

➢ Actions – connecting, envisioning

➢ Outcome – cooperation

➢ Key words – concepts, innovation, potential, creativity, possibilities

➢ Cultures – France, R&D, project leadership, younger generation (why are we doing it, asking questions as a norm)

Process Style

➢ Energy – moving at, debating

➢ Actions – proposing, reasoning

➢ Outcome – solution

➢ Key words – facts, details, procedure, observation, proof, planning, analysis

➢ Cultures – central Europe, engineering, accounting, oil and chemicals, government, manufacturing, pharma

Action Style

➢ Energy – moving against, bargaining

➢ Actions – demanding, exchanging

➢ Outcome – deal

➢ Key words – results, objectives, performance, deals, challenges, decisions

➢ Cultures – US, Australia, sales, retail, consumer goods, senior managers

Thank you for your time, I hope you found this guide useful.

We covered the prime approach for How to master Leadership and Influence in Teams. Using the concepts presented in this book will enhance and develop your skills so you are able to get what, how, and when you need it in the future... I am happy to answer your questions. Feel free to contact me @ m.nir@sapir-cs.com

----

About the Author

Michael Nir, Transformation Inspiration Expert, Lean Agile Coach; empowers organizations to deliver results;

With over sixteen years of experience Michael has been leading change at global organizations in diverse industries. Committed to sustained results as well as the journey, Michael balances a passion for creativity and innovation alongside tested proven approaches for solution delivery. Michael inspires people and teams to change, cognitively and emotionally, building on enthusiasm from climbing the hill AND reaching the top.

In his toolbox are: agile product development and Scrum, project management know how, Lean Startup and Lean Agile expertise, change leadership and team building experience, and pragmatically integrating theory into practice.

Combining a BSc in Civil and MSc in Industrial Engineering from the prestigious Technion Institute of Technology, Michael aggregates technical acumen with study and practice of Gestalt therapy and Instrumental Enrichment, a philosophy of mediated learning. His clients represent a multitude of industries: Hi-tech, Banking, IT, Software, Health, Petrochemical and Infrastructure.

Sharing his knowledge and experience, Michael authored 10 bestsellers on Influencing, Lean Agile, Teams, and Leadership. The books engage readers in learning and motivate personal transformation.

Made in the USA
Middletown, DE
23 February 2019